SHABDAGUCHHA
An International Bilingual Poetry Magazine

I0172912

26 Years of Publication

**This issue presented
Poets from Seventeen Countries**

Shabdaguchha
Published by Shabdaguchha Press

Shabdaguchha

Vol. 26 No. 3/4   January - December 2024 $10

Editor: Hassanal Abdullah   হাসানআল আব্দুল্লাহ
Advisor: Jyotirmoy Datta   জ্যোতির্ময় দত্ত
                         Joan Digby   জোন ডিগবি

Assistant Editor: Naznin Seamon   নাজনীন সীমন

Consulting Editor: Shameem Chawdhury (BD)

Correspondents: Peter Thabit Jones (UK)
                         Prabir Das, Chandan Das (India)

Special Correspondent:
                         Romel Rahman, Roni Adhikari (Dhaka)

Shabdaguchha, a Bilingual (Bengali-English) Poetry Magazine, Published by the editor, from Shabdaguchha Press. Subscription rate is $12 per year in the United States and $15 in other countries. To subscribe, please send check or money order in US Dollar payable to Shabdaguchha.
All correspondence and subscriptions should be addressed to the editor:
Shabdaguchha, 85-22 85th street, Woodhaven, NY 11421, USA.
Phone: (718) 849 2617 E-mail: habdu056@aol.com
                                shabdaguchha@gmail.com
Web Site: http://www.shabdaguchha.com

Shabdaguchha accepts submission throughout the whole year. Poetry, written in Bengali, English or translated from any language to these two languages, is always welcome. Book reviews and news on poets and poetry could also be sent. Each submission should be accompanied by a short bio of the author. E-mail submissions are more appreciated, but Bengali written in English alphabet is not acceptable.

Shabdaguchha Press
Woodhaven, New York
ISSN 1531-2038
ISBN 978-1-7330285-6-1
Cover Art: Joan Harrison

Contents:

This issue featured poets from the following countries:

Austria Bangladesh Czech Republic Germany Greece
Guatemala Hungary India Iran Italy Mexico Netherlands
Norway Poland Sweden Ukraine USA

Editorial:

26 YEARS OF SHABDAGUCHHA

When we started editing *Shabdaguchha*, we did not think of its longevity, nor did we have any idea of including poets from different countries. But, as we are publishing the 26th anniversary issue, we can gladly say our involvement with poets from around the world is significant. The number of submissions we receive, the international platform we created, and the poetic richness we encountered over the years are simply outstanding. Friendships among poets from different parts of the world have been a major achievement of *Shabdaguchha* and we will make serious effort to continue enhancing that, since fruitful poetic exchange between nations can bring viable peace to all societies.

We also established Shabdaguchha International Poetry Award in 2001. Every two years we choose one poet from the magazine's pages to honor the award. There has been a four-member jury board, and each member is required to nominate three poets. Whoever gets the highest nomination would receive the prize. In 2023, the honorarium for the prize was five hundred dollars and a crest. The award went to polish poet Kazimierz Burnet. Among the other winners are Amir Or (2021), Dariusz Tomasz Lebioda (2019), Peter Thabit Jones (2017), Sambhu Rakshit (2013) and more.

No publication is easy, especially after the pandemic the cost of everything tripled. Nevertheless, we keep on publishing the magazine on two platforms: printed and online. To minimize the expenses, we are now publishing only one issue per year and will continue to do that. Poets, especially the emerging ones, would highly be recommended to read the magazine, at least from the online version, to have a clear idea of what type of poetry we publish, before submitting their work. However, we still want to give more emphasis to publishing emerging poets as they are the future of world poetry.

Bengt O Björklund

YOU CAN NEVER HOLD ME DOWN

you can never hold me down
with your fierce fire folding lethargy
I knew your tempting water too well
you tried to snap me bold late one night
running like a tree in full storm I bellowed
but your track-stopped me dead
in time for my eyes to dye my world

lemmings' stream into cliff absolution
trees go root wise in a communion with yesterday
there is no time for fake funerals
when strange fruit hang in old trees
elementary is pure dereliction down
a translation of so much wrong
put into a hot pot in the middle of the night

Sweden

Manfred Chobot

20 KILOS AGO I STOPPED DANCING

some want
to sleep with Kerouac
others rather with Bukowski
some prefer Ginsberg
or are crazy
about Capote
pine away for
Gide, Rimbaud, Verlaine—

In the meantime, they doze listlessly
somewhere
and masturbate until
their bad conscience runs
out of their spinal cord

or they cry
for fifteen minutes
the whole night
or even for months
without stopping the tears and snot

perhaps this is how
the great flood came about

Translated from the German by Karoline Ruhdorfer

Austria

William Heyen

SKYROS

Decades ago I stood where in the ancient texts Odysseus
    visited Achilles,

told him he must not waste his time here lest his sword rust
    & his flesh become

a sheep's—he must partake of Agamemnon's war. For a few
seconds
    in that storied place

scented with brine, I became present within Odysseus's
plaintive tone,
    flashes of Achilles' shield

& tongue—then I returned to my cruise ship half-spelled, half-
sated
    with belief again.

Brockport/New York

Kazimeriz Burnat

PILIGRIME

where are you going, human
your steps are slow
and gait sluggish

from hospital to hospital
you bite into the centre of pain
into the wilderness of torment

from night to night
you search in vain for the bottom line
in everything that surrounds you

an angel beyond the horizon
draws the contours of your face
you stare at the ground
your legs rest against the sky
you look for wisdom in this
what is not

open the book
on the blank page
begin a new chapter
with an exclamation mark

FATHER

mother was waiting
for your last touch
you didn't believe
and the death certificate for you
was unbelievable

your unseeing eyes
and wise eyelids
still reveal everything
which makes sense
sometimes towers without symbols
headless pedestals

my prayer
is a stone from my heart
redemption of souls
of both of you

my memory
is life
of the three of us

SOLITARY TREAT

Good is a pass
to the fullness of life
it multiplies what you have
enough for others
and even more—
changes chaos into order
unity into multiplicity
a meal into a feast
a stranger into a friend

gratitude
enriches the past
brings peace into the present
and creates a vision of tomorrow—
ingratitude
releases evil

Translated from the Polish by Alicja Maria Kuberska

তীর্থযাত্রী

মানুষ তুমি যাচ্ছো কোথায়
এলোমেলো ধীর পায়ে?

হাসপাতাল থেকে হাসপাতালে
তীব্র ব্যথা কামড়ে ধরে
যন্ত্রণায় কুঁকড়ে গিয়ে

রাত থেকে অন্য রাতে
চতুর্পাশের সমস্তটা তন্নতন্ন
করছো তুমি অযথাই, অকারণে

দিগন্তের অন্যপাশে
দেবদূত এক
তোমার মুখের ছবি আঁকে
ঊর্ধ্বাকাশে দুই পা তুলে
মাটির দিকে তাকিয়ে তুমি
বোধ ও জ্ঞানের চাবি খোঁজো।

জীবন বইয়ের নতুন পাতায়
নতুন শুরু অধ্যায়েতে
বিস্ময়ের চিহ্ন দিয়ে
নতুন করে শুরু করো।

বাবা

তোমার শেষ স্পর্শের জন্য
অধীর অপেক্ষায় ছিলেন মা
অথচ তুমি বিশ্বাস করোনি তা
আর তোমার মৃত্যু সনদও ছিলো
একান্তই অবিশ্বাস্য

দর্শনক্ষমতাহীন তোমার চোখ
সাথে অভিজ্ঞতাভারাবনত চোখের পাতা
এখনও সমস্তটাই ব্যক্ত করে
ভীষণ অর্থবহ সব
কখনও কখনও

10

আমার প্রার্থনা
যেনো হৃদয়নিসৃত জমাট পাথরখণ্ড

নির্জনতার কাব্য

ভালো মানে জীবন জুড়ে তৃপ্তিসুখের
সোনার সেই চাবি
কেবলই তা বাড়ায় আনন্দসম্ভার–যা যা আছে যতোটুকু
হয়তো বহু বহুগুণে
চরম নৈরাজ্যকেও ভালো কেবল
সুসংযত শৃঙ্খলার সীমান্তে দাঁড় করাতে পারে অনায়াসে
ঠিক যেমন পারে একতাকে বহুতায়,
দিনের সাধারণ খাবারকে রাজকীয় ভোজ
আর অচেনাকে নিমেষে বন্ধুতে পরিণত করতে

কৃতজ্ঞতাবোধ
অতীতকে অতিক্রান্ত করে
শান্তির সুবাতাসে ভরে দেয় বর্তমান
এবং আগামীর প্রশস্ত দরজা খুলে দেয় অনায়াসে–
অকৃজ্ঞতা অন্য দিকে
অশুভকে আহ্বান করে উদাত্ত কণ্ঠে

Translated into Bengali by Naznin Seamon

Poland

Laura Gravaglia

YUSUF

Yusuf is sitting next to his mother, his body lying faceup
in the field.
Sunshine's carving his childlike gaze.
In the morning lightening in the sky, a blast:
perhaps a thunderstorm, but no rain
melting the soil into endless dark rivulets.
War deletes the borders of sense.
Perhaps it was a game, his mother had been sleeping
for hours, her arms folded on her belly
and wouldn't wake up.
And the black chasm had swallowed
the poor things of home.
Yusuf still doesn't know, his father
and his brother killed far away
beyond the dunes of blood
from sunrise to sunset.
His mother had been telling
tales of love, tales of peace.
Yusuf is now waiting for her voice.

END

It thawed into the silence of a farewell,
time, which slipped through our fingers,
burnt down to ashes.
And it was not only the words,
the piled-up things
which shut memory in the furrow,
life's deep wrinkle,
two planks nailed on our heart.

Translated from the Italian by Annarita Tavani
Italy

George Wallace

LIGHTNING, LIGHTNING

control yourself, they said, but I could not; there are other urges
I obey; the wind that swings the lantern; the rain that shakes the
sawgrass; the great stone that grinds corn down by the bushel,
where the river falls;

control yourself, they said, but I could not, for there are other
urges I obey; the truth unstrung, that disguises itself as legend
and shears the heart like a scything knife; the wound unhealed,
that disguises itself as law and lives many lifetimes and makes a
mockery of youth;

the primal fire, that burns like an unholy kiss and has no name
except fire; and lightning, lightning, which strikes and strikes
the willow, and lights the darkness surrounding you and me;

(and the grinding stone shall crush the corn and make liquor of
grain; and the river shall declare itself in the newborn's cry; and
the wind shall resurrect itself in the widower's eye and express
itself in love's new caresses);

control yourself, they said, but I could not, there are other urges
I obey;

the cowbell in the mowing field, the soul in its shallow grave
that plucks the lyre; the revolutionary herald that waits just
below surfaces and prepares to burst forth and ring anew, like a
sweet storm in spring;

and the shepherd with his flock, who knows much and says
little, and holds his tongue 'til shearing time, like a shy child in
primary school who finally raises his hand in triumph, having
known the answer all along.

LOOKING THRU THE MASQUE OF DEATH

I see children of the field in their white working blouses who
sing in wheat and carry socialist machetes into capitalist
sugarcane and ignore the inconsistencies and sing look at me
look at me like crickets in trees and study the textbook of the
stars and they would die if they had to sing alone;

I see tenement children in their slacks and blue jersies who sing
in milk and run up and down applecart stairs and capture the
flag and make a hella racket near chimneypots tb wards and
grand hotel parking garages, for whom shaking down the man is
a gumball machine and not a crime and water mixes with oil
and life is not up for debate it's holy! and they would die if they
had to sing alone;

I see the children of the boulevard, and the children of gypsies
and seafaring men and bikers, in their traveling clothes, who
dream on Gulf Coast shores and collect love like Great Lake
driftwood, and share tattoos and build bonfires that touch the
moon and never look back; and children of Greenwood
Mississippi who sing in cotton in their stay at home clothes,
how they throw seductive eyes at each other all summer behind
the general store, and gather kindling wood by the fork road
when winter sets in, and they slice up the night like a river of
gold and they share the gold;

Here's to them all! children in lonely windows, Navajo corn
children, postage stamp children, children after a long drive
home; children of the bleachers and factory whistle, children of
the grandee and the satrap, children of the holy sativa and the
refugee camp; Ethiopian children, London children, children of
Nicaragua and the Faeroes and the Americas and the fog,
children of wild horsemen on the fast uproarious Asian plateau,
children of the soul and savannah and the heavenly oceanic surf
cloud, clothed in innocence and opportunity;

14

I see them all! through the masque of death, children of
children, folksingers and handclappers and dancers and players
at the grass harp, in their hand me down shoes, or no shoes at
all; in rice fields and golden temples, on football pitches and in
the delicate gardens of Versailles, on tarmacs and slipping
conspiratorially among the redwoods, negotiating the dubious
seductions of Inwood, New York; who would die if they had to
sing their song alone;

And in the gloomy European shadows, carrying black and white
Bibles and textbooks and fulfilling promises to Science or God,
children holed up in laboratories and philosophical towers and
academic halls, cooking up principles and certainties and
devotions that will surely rescue every suffering thing in this
world from itself, including themselves;

Children of commerce
Children of peace
Who sing in milk
Who sing in wheat
Here's to them all

I would sing with them all, I would die with them all, if they
had to sing their song alone

New York/USA

Shankha Ghosh

MY FACE IS BURIED AMONG BILLBOARDS

Being all alone I am standing
for you at the corner of the lane
brooding I will show my face
but it's buried among billboards!

Just a simple dialogue or two
I will exchange in a blink of an eye
but it's lost in the glare of the glamorous
billboards, utterly colorful.

How would we dare to see each other
is quite difficult to comprehend
hail on my exaggeration
hail too my own motherland.

The expression of the eyes is traded,
inextricably mingled with you
in neon light that produces a commodity—
nothing left as personal, nothing is private.

The words I have spoken remained lonely
being left at the corner of the lane
only the weary mask of mine
is hanging on a billboard.

Translated from the Bengali by Kamrul Hassan

India

Bengt Berg

TO CARRY

To carry is perhaps what life is all about:
the wood that warms through the winter,
the thoughts that make us lift off with
our feet still on the ground, the respect for
what is around us, the grief that also takes
its place—and all this longing. But also
what is not as beautiful: the anger, the hatred,
the jealousy; or the toothache, the shame,
the guilt. We carry everything in the basket
of life: our joy, our worry, our sorrow and our love.

EVENING

How many evenings should be counted
to make up a whole night?

Even today the crow spotted me
from his position at the top of the birch tree.

The invisible music behind
the birch's light-colored grid

Turning a thought in the center
And once more; from the silence

the sap seeps even though
it is the 7th of February

With and against the sun,
even the shadow in the snow

Goes with it across the lake
in the air that cools towards evening

Sweden

17

Thomas Möhlmann

MOTHER

Mother come out of the tree
with your thread and all day
there's been no one to talk to no bird
snared and on the table inside

two empty plates two warm glasses
without wine and here your poor chair
all alone without you don't you see so
come out of that tree dear mother out

the chimney no smoke under the kettle
no fire and the goat filled to bursting
is nibbling on the rug by the door and the chicken
lies there like a bouquet of dried flowers

and when I dropped the vase the pieces
scattered everywhere and in my mouth
everything just grows sweeter and already around you
there's a swaying and creaking under the full sky

so come little mother come out of that tree
with your thread and your tins, with both your legs.

Translated from the Dutch by Judith Wilkinson

WE WILL

Definitely, my love, they will, but we will do more, they
are going to, but with playful ease; we are going to do it,

even more: they don't have any chance at all because we

will have more, none of us live longer than eighty years on
average

not them and not us, but you will see, my love, what we
will still be able to wring out of those forty years or so, while
they

ah, they are still going to and they will, over a hundred years
for all I care, and still no more than what they themselves will

all the birds that stretch their wings at once, not to fly
but out of pure fright, they will, my love, just like us

but before it comes to that, we will, we will, as planned, as
intended
down that whole row of blessed years left to us, that we will.

Translated from the Dutch by David Colmer

Netherlands

Attila Szabó Palócz

DON'T TELL A WORD

Enjoy the silence
hunt on the words only in your mind
and if you get lost
clench your teeth in the fist

in the shadow of fleeting summers
crystals are rolling down on the slope
blocking the way of the coquettish earthworms
only the same old smile remained
on the trail of disappearing fragments of memories

the memories will have compensation in goodness
and I'm smells again on the forthcoming sleepless night . . .
in the glare of the crystals
and through the maze on the slopes
on the long way of troubles
I reach to tirelessness . . .

it's not worth looking back
and maybe it is already too late to looking back
because here everything is so easily fleeting, like summers
and so gloomy, as duty
and it seems that there are no more convenient privileges

instead of privileges you can expect a ransom
instead of the words quietness
instead of noise silence
until you recognize your yesterday's selfness in the rearview
mirror
your confused selfness
disappointed
shyly

with the purest lights
in the glare of the crystal
as you roll down the slopes
on the light trail
irrevocably

your yesterday's irrevocable selfness
today is already screaming for help
because you no longer follow his path
and perceive it as betrayal

your yesterday's irrevocable selfness
today is already screaming for help
—but not to you

SHYNESS

I only address you shyly in this prayer.
I will not take your name on my lips without reason.
I'm just shyly sneaking around the years
that are piling up on my biography.
I'm shyly scolding the neighbor's dog
with quiet words I make him grind his teeth,
to recoil, to retreat
into hopelessness . . .
I sit shyly by the campfire,
I shyly grab the bottle that is circulating around,
I grab your hair timidly . . .
I choose my words carefully so that my words do not reach you
deep down
within you
on the peaks of your soul . . .

Yet you know perfectly that my shyness is only a facade,
a mask for my insecurity,
a swallow cries through the scenery,

21

our endless minds tucked away in fur,
gut-wrenching comfort penetrates to the bone,
handbooks on forestry describe my character
as I am laying in the mud
by the lake,
maybe in Bakonyszücs,
or anywhere else in the world . . .
either our world is too big,
or you are too little in it,
a little approach,
your stream-existence is a candle wick
whose flame is reflected on the water's surface,
waving and flaming all at once . . .
you are flaming water,
a crumbling balcony,
a bouquet of water scavenger beetles,
a decaying look,
a ladder to the sky,
Absolution and Elevation into the blinding light,
fate daring to the end all registers,
swaying shadow
in a space stripped of dimensions . . .
a swaying shadow in our blood, stripped of dimensions . . .

I only address you shyly in this prayer,
and please let my shyness be
not only worthy
but also a truly protective and shielding disguise to be,
when I will live through face to face
in all my obsolete fears,
the flames and the absolution,
the relish and the brave,
the always encouraged locks
as they wrap around my fingers as I timidly stroke your hair...

Translated from the Hungarian by the poet
Hungary

Sara Ehsan

IS THERE A PLACE

1.
is there a place
to collect bombed dreams
is there a dialog
of the dead
do they still exist?
Wounds from which
light streams out
do they still exist?
body parts growing together
do they still exist?
laughing faces
in the reflection of a mirror
do they still exist?
encouraging poems
words that hit harder than bombs
We write words in black ink
across the stream of red dreams
Some suffocate in secret
under the weight of broken dreams
some wither under the force of
silence
shadowy times
amputated words
bleeding sentences
how to write a poem
when it only
documents abysses?

2.
"When the unspeakable is brought to light, it is political."
                                        —Annie Ernaux

Our backs
facing the sea
in expectation
of nothing

the beach stands
empty
longing for
the storm

the revolutionary guards
transform themselves
into people
laughing and joking
with us

a sound springs
from the shell
with the first
thought of the day:
They were executed.

Lead on
our eyelids
the thought
"to go to work"
absurd

We mourn
through the day
in our ears
the sound

of screaming
mothers
frenetically
dancing
at their
children's graves

we send
"stories"
into the world
consisting of
four intersecting
straight lines
before the execution
unknowing during it
and afterwards

the senselessness
sponges us
into a morass
with a system

the reproduction
of martyrs
victims
butchers
and their
reversal

at the bottom
we sink
earthly
idle
accomplices

in between

organizing the children's birthday party
if there was
something
to celebrate
except
being alive

we have been procrastinating
for decades
creating illusions
of community
and
yes, what?

of unity
while we
rot
and the spark
in the air
extinguishes
the flame

Iran

Svitlana Breslavska

YOU WOKE UP

you woke up
the moon is shining in your window
and on the bed lies a fish
with the sparkly slippery scales
and blinks at you
with her round eye

O fish be my wife
I will put a ring on you
I will be faithful to you
till your next
spawning

the fish sighed
and became
your cradle

***
you set the rules:
not to call
not to tell anybody
not to suffer

you draw borders for me:
me, limitless
you want to limit—
to cram the wind
into a bottle!
yet I only live by one rule—
to love you

Translated from the Ukrainian by Oksana Lutsyshyna
Ukraine

Joan Digby

SUNSET

After a fiery sunset
exploded on the mountains,
then yielded to a pink dusk,
Orion stood on his head last night
in a black southern sky.

WAITING FOR THE DRAGONFLIES

Not five minutes in the garden
gloves, hat, and netting all in place
mosquitoes find a chink
in the armor and draw blood

Safely inside, looking out
through the windows
we await the arrival of dragonflies
the air force of glittering wings that will
pluck mosquitoes as they whirl
and dance their lethal aerial ballet

DAY STAR

Summer in Alaska
sunset comes before dawn
at midnight pink clouds
cover the sky among black trees
and soon the day star beds down
to catch a few hours of sleep
before she wakes just after three
calling out her name, Aurora
as she rises

Oyster Bay/USA

Vera Kopecka

WATER

I am water
which slipped through your fingers
when you wanted a drink

Injuring oneself on stones
runs between the shores
and falls into your hands

It falls and falls
on your back

Stroke the water
it will be yours
squeeze
it will disappear

THE WELL

Loneliness is a well
bottomless
Cool water
fresh transparent

Sip it
priceless
in the heat of the day

Woe to that
it will fall into the well

Translated from the Czech by Gwidon Hefid
Czech Republic

Piter Prokopjak

DYSTHYMIA

In autumn stars descend down the leaves to
the streets passing through me rocking
with the wind's pulse weaves baste cumulated
worlds I would like to forget the pupils
betray me liquefying wax
houses holding on to a mother's hem
mists suck moisture cracked
chestnuts I arrange in the satchel before
the boiling roundabout discus flies away
on Freedom Square like taxies back then
flee from standstill through rushed
evenings all joints let go
sense sticks with elastic
sinusoid smoke supports households
captive mixed with silence
my present future pasts

IN THE SUMMER OF 1985

we were sitting on an overpass
swinging our legs
inhaling evening
below flickered greedy caterpillars
biting hastily
into mature sun
warmed up lupine flowed through meadows
blurring the day to the last
light seed
we did not feel pain
secrets lured us
and faith in beauty

transformed into a bird
took our gazes away
to the abysmal vaultings
from where there is no return

Translated from the Polish by Kristin Kilde

Poland

Roberto Mendoza-Ayala

WINTER

Nothing happens in white nothingness.
It blew her wild hair as she went.
In the blindness that illuminates
silent I came to the house again.

A flock of sleepy birds fluttering
along the road to earth, the snow, the ground;
nothing in the high nests, only the drizzle
that the frosty air had promised me.

Is the brandished sword of lightning
a piercing blade? The blue of the void.
Yet something happens: grayish footprints.
Now I was a first winter ago.

THE FEATHER

A feather floats on the random
and traces its mark on shimmering waves.
Like a delicate comb,
in its swing it spins yarns,

temporary clouds, baroque
foams tangled
among the myriad of diagonal
lines that make it up.

In its wave-like wandering
it struggles tirelessly
transmuted into a lonely oar,
the ghost of a wing.

A challenging sign
in the silence,
this scrapped sail
is the distant echo of a bird's cry

which on the surface
of the tide shines
as a castaway,
arrowless crest of light.

The evanescent white flame
crowns the ocean in its drift
when in a fleeting moment
it reaches the peak of the sea.

New York/USA

Silvia Kofler

PERIPATETIC

Our toes hurt
because she moves to
some loud rock beat.

Years ago she made
us pose in St. Cast Brittany,
at France's North coast
to draw us
in pencil strokes.

Three decades later
she posed us to paint
us for another portrait
in Kansas City, Missouri.

Who knows,
maybe she will want to
pose us for a sculpture
next time.

Who knows
where that may be.

Does she think she can abuse us
just like years ago.
We may just go on strike
and refuse to move her.

POSTAL

Slapping the self-stick stamps
onto fifty envelopes suggests
just how terrible it must be
to perform
one task over and over . . .

I dawdle to
observe other customers
in the self-service lobby at the post office,
delight at the observation that just about
every other individual double-checks the mail slot
(I tend to double-check)
after dropping mail,
just to make sure.

Just to make sure.
Forced to double-check
every day
for eight hours
may turn any worker
postal.

Kansas City/USA

Barbara Orlowski

SHADOWS

Sculptured shadows on the sand
they will remain in memory

the white wings of angels touch the heart
and white lilies in the garden

dust-covered memories
they are beginning to live again

dreams have remained only in dreams
they are constantly dreaming about being fulfilled

and the shadows will remain on the sand a memory

TIME

where dreams come true in full magic
they have a taste for passion

and the whispers of angels
they touch the top of the mountains slightly

where stones carved in the
shade—they are silent

where moments smell of delight
and you have other hands in your hands

longing has become the motto of life
wisdom suits sarcasm

despite the dusty clocks
you know—time is running out fast

MAGIC

I paint my imagination with a brush
at sunrise in golden rays
the wind spiked the smell of tea roses
coconut sweet pineapple and orange
I am waiting for the beach sun-warmed
sand grains and shells are pouring through my hands
the ocean quietly roars murmurs and plays
music caresses words in dreams and dreams
and only the hummingbirds above the flowers
hung in the air

FLOWERS KISS THE SKY

When the flowers kiss the sky
you are walking in the summer time
by the seashore
wet sand caresses your feet
and the sun blows bright tresses
in colorful ribbons
only the wind lightly dances on the wave
sways red roses
in your garden
muslin floral dress
gently emphasizes the shapes of the figure
in a sunny day
because when flowers kiss the sky
blue butterflies are hugging you
like in a magical dream

Translation from the Polish by Dariusz Tomasz Lebioda
Germany

Maria Lisella

LEAVES

Even when loneliness overtakes me
and I imagine I will never get up, I do.
Trees and leaves fill my 7th story windows
so close I can nearly touch them, close

enough that I can watch the squirrels
scamper as if their goals were to simply
ride the wind with the leaves slapping
their furry rumps and tails that sashay

from gray branch to gray branch; they play
and as much as I see them as urban rats
and pests, their tiny faces, and rapid fire
movements entertain me and then I realize

I am quite alive whether I want to be or not
no one ever told me I had to like this new life
of mine or that I even had to live it, but there
it is like the unsuspecting squirrels, I heed

the swish of leaves in the morning, knowing dry
breezes will follow, the sun will dapple
my shoulders, I may not hear a human voice
until I rise, dress and go out to meet the wind.

A SHORT FALL

I thought it was a bird landing on the air conditioner
or the urban doves romancing on the fire escape.
I could not identify the hushed thud like a
not a bird body but a bouquet of puffy aloe
fingers, swollen with healing gel and kindness.

Am surprised it made any sound at all. All at once
I am alerted to what must be done for the usually
silent plant; for our future together: my scrapes
and burns would follow. I will need this plant
to yield its sticky matter, so I preserve it, re-plant
it, secure it into the soil, keep it erect, yet allow
it to drape ballerina style off the side of the terracotta
pot my mother-in-law rimmed with daisies,
not a pot I would have chosen but it holds
this life that does not give up; this life that took
a short fall to the honey-colored floor, visible and audible
enough to be rescued. I tuck the lesson inside where
my grief is visible, audible, yet find no aloe for the heart.

HOUSE PLANTING

Powered by people, memories and fed
by the bachelor on the 7th floor when I am
away. He says he knows nothing about them
yet each time I return, they are flourishing.

White lily-like palms sprout on the ends
of a mass of upturned leaves in prayer crowding
the largest pot, the last project my husband and his best
friend completed . . . moving the smaller plant

to a larger terracotta pot facing east.
Peace plants are so well-tuned
to overheated NY apartments, can live
side by side in silence mostly, the aloe

plant with its full and juicy fingers grows
willy-nilly, sometimes a branch drops to
the floor with its many fingers but it does not
die. It waits for me to lift it, replace it where

it can go on living with its siblings . . . nearby
is the pothos that climbs up a chopstick,
that originally arrived from a Chinese
restaurant. Set in a handmade grey

clay pot with a rough saucer to capture
overflow, the earthiest of the brood.
Named for Johann, the beautiful boy
who took his own life in an apartment

in Brooklyn. His parents retired to Florida.
Their grief pulled them further home
to Colombia where they re-planted roots
amid the tangle of their ancestors' land.

Couched and safe from this harsh modern
America with so much promise but left them
childless. My Johann plant never grows past
a certain height. Each year I send a photo

of it to his parents to let them know he is
not forgotten. Next to Johann is Leonid
in a vase of pebbles a sprig of a Peace Plant
rises after his Ukrainian parents fled the

U.S. because, they too, were afraid to lose
their children to modern America, the
land of promise and pathos, a place where
you can lose your dreams, and your children.

New York/USA

Fatemeh Ekhtesari

SHE IS NOT A WOMAN

5
I slowly remove my clothes
Take them off one by one
Under my shirt there is a battlefield
A depot of ammunition and guns

Naked, like a beginning
Naked, like a bloody knife
Naked, like a forbidden poem
Like the one you're reading now

I slowly remove my books
From the shelves one by one
The dead heroes rise
Stake their claim on me

Hafez and Eliot's sleazy stares
Weary Samsa's scaly hands
Don Quixote and Ali Baba's twisted cocks
A rape of deaf ears

My skin is a frayed cover
Line by line *Regarding the Pain of Others*
The world is a cellar
Slaughterhouse-Five

Grief is the title of everything written
Happiness is a footnote
365 days of suffering
365 nights of Sodom

Come, pour petrol into my mouth

Come, burn down the library
Detonate the lump in my throat
Empty yourself on me

13

Far away, a lamp flickers
A flame suffocates in thick smog
On these most fly-like of days
I hit my head against the pane in vain
Blood-red streaks of news on the laptop
Blood-red streaks of news on the TV
Where else can she go but the news
She who's buried on the wrong side of a border

The woman filled with dreams of return
Stares at the screen and waits for Godot
Her mother tongue swells in her throat
In Beckett's grip, she gasps for air
Her lips don't hold back the cries for freedom
My lips crack with swallowed words
Your lips are covered with blood from the batons
The pain echoes within my body

I'm drenched to the bone; do the drowned sleep
I'm tying my wandering leg to the bed
I've been banished to a far-away island
And someone has swallowed the map
The lamp, the sun's hope at night
Is slowly going out
Where else can she go but the news
She who is trapped in cubes

*Translated from Persian by Mohammad M. Izadi, Johanne
Fronth-Nygren, and Matthew Rana*

Norway

Isidoros Karderinis

WE PLANTED

We planted our seeds in the clouds
And instead of roses the rain germinated.

We planted our footprints on the sand
And instead of light the sun burned us.

We planted our dreams in the sea
And instead of serenity the waves drifted us away.

THE PLUCKING

I remember when we were kids
In our carelessness
We were plucking margaritas.

Now, in life's hole
We are plucking the nights with moon.

Greece

John Burroughs

WHERE WOULD THE MOMENT BE?

It's a messy question
depending on which
moment and what one
means by be

One would expect a god
to have the answer
though they appear
to need a moment
Bogged down
and scattered
on earth as it is

Where would the moment be
besides in the moment?
In the future or past or both?

Somewhere a war or several
have occurred or will
because when
have they not
or will they not
and what is a moment
for if not peace?
Spinning wheels
and recalibrating
on earth as it is

What if such a god
was a moment
and the moment
has passed?

WHAT IF THIS IS THE LAST POEM I EVER WRITE AND IT'S NOT FINISHED?

I.

Because I don't know what to write anymore
or actually I do, I have many things to write
and many reasons not to bother writing them

My mother is dead and I am in between
her birthdate April 27th and her death May 5th
and a baby was born into our family less
than one week later on my first post-mom
Mother's Day when the last thing I wanted
to do was celebrate and the last place I wanted
to go was back to the hospital though there
were many other places I wished to go back
into and though that happened eleven years ago
a growing boy still reminds me of Mother's Day
and orphanhood and his mother may not get it
though now her mother, my wife, is dead too
and maybe she gets it for her but not me
because how can we ever get anything
for anyone else when we can
barely, if ever, get ourselves?

And don't get me
started on fathers

II.
D.R. Wagner is dead
and so are Jim Lang and David Berman
and William Merricle and Prince
and Jack McGuane and Terry Provost
and Gil-Scott Heron and somehow
even Stephen Dunn and somehow
I got started on fathers after all

But isn't that where it all starts?

III.
At least that's what the Bible said
though it didn't call god father till Exodus 4
and before that god was Elohim, plural
the original they/them, until the patriarchy
refused to use their preferred pronouns

IV.
My mother is dead and I am in between
living and dying and trying and giving up

And the first person I heard say "success
has many fathers but failure is an orphan"
was Oliver North but he got it from J.F.K.
who tweaked it from Il Duce's son-in-law
who seems to have paraphrased Tacitus
and I am an orphan with many fathers
and only one mother and I have plenty
to write about and rage about but rage
is all about and people are dying
on every side and—heavy sigh—despite
the best efforts of every better poet than I
our children continue to die

And how can I
let it all end here?

Ohio/USA

David Mills

SPEED BOY [1]

[*In 1938, a Teenage, Harry Stewart Jr. goes to see the Hollywood film "Test Pilot" in his Corona, Queens neighborhood.*]

Walked down 104th 'til I ran out of it, hooked a left then a right, was right back on it, smack-dab at the drab Plaza Theater, under the cherry-pop letters bare-knuckled on its marquee: *Test*

Pilot starring Clark Gable as Jim Lane and Spencer Tracy as Gunner—Lane's two-bit gum-smacking sidekick, right there in the glassed-in movie poster with the blue background, Tracy—

in a bone dome—interrogated the heavens while Clark squinted at eye level. Nearly tumbling over my red shoelaces, I plunked down forty cents, swung open a scuffed glass door for my

buddy Tim who'd just showed up. Hello Saturday matinee! We were in, inside the double-theater's marble lobby, with another movie poster smearing a sandwich board beneath

the winking, acorn-shaped chandelier. Even though I'd smuggled a Baby Ruth between one ankle and an argyle, I still drifted over the concession stand, where hanging from the lights,

were photos of Hollywood stars framed by heavenly stars, popcorn trapped and spread like a golden seashore in a glass cabinet. I settled on Twizzlers and a buttered tub of corn kernels.

In the back of the auditorium, folks' heads were bundled up in Chesterfield smoke as we made our way down the side aisle. Not noticing, I plopped down where one plush seat had vanished,

stung my butt bone, parted ways. with half a bucket.

III. WORLD WAR II WARMUP

I read *Flying Aces* in the 1930s so I could
soar in the 1940s. Cause, even if nobody
in those stories looked like me, flipping

through that flying pulp was my World
War II warmup. And stretched out on
my bed, staring at the wrinkled blue paint

on my ceiling, my eyes ballooned by enthusiasm
and air, back then and there, I knew
I would live what had never existed.

New York/USA

***NOTE 1: Speed Boy**—a high-top sneaker worn by males in the 1930s*

Dimitris P. Kraniotis

MINUS ONE

I pulled the earth
To cover us
Just in case we might wear tonight
Disarming and bloodless
The words we spat out yesterday
Like seeds

But don't answer me hasty
Wait your turn
In line
I'm waiting for answers
From you and from me
Again and again

Up until yesterday
Until reaching the certainity and unexpected
—One of the elevators
Basement indefinitely
And inexorably with anger
(Which logic was rented
From my imagination tonight?)

But I don't want the mud
To ferment our bodies
Filling with minus one tomorrow
Roots of lotus and myths

THE RED POEM

I painted red
The sky
Days that I lost myself
And denied myself
Laughing without reason
I lived those

I painted red
The water
I drowned in tears
And saved me
Forgetting my guilt
I cheated myself

I painted in red
This poem
With words I erased myself
And resurrected myself
Writing in blood
I avenged myself

Greece

Rudy Alfonzo Gomez Rivas

ON THE SEASHORE

I have come from faraway lands
carrying on my shoulders
nebulae that transgress
the reluctance and stupor of thorns and pus.

I walk to the rhythm of the horizon
silencing fables
that offer naked dawns.

In me the frost mirrors
shatter the gait
that has been left hanging
in yellow windows.

Incense is a distant scent
where it nests the childish voice
of figs and broken birds.

At the seashore:
a dream
a smile
some laborious hands
some lips that invite madness
a song by Serrat
a girl opening her wings in the face of fear
some eyes inventing another country.

MASKS

We build masks, pretend to reach the center of the root and its mysteries.We build masks, seduce death and its corsairs.

We build masks, the echo of the cetaceans is suicidal on the lips.

We build masks, the jade's insurrection paints crucifixes on our temples.

We build masks, hirsute stones paint doubts on our hands.

We build masks, white spells annihilate dreams and entangle tomorrow.

root
      death
            cetaceans
                  jade
                      stones
                          spells are what we finally
                                  turn out to be.

THE DOOR, BLACKBERRY OF DREAMS

Son,
the doors create dialogues between life and death.

The door's bolt is an eye that watches the laughter.

The hinges angels with their aluminum song
rule the daily defeats.

The keys save us from the whip of the streets.

An old woman paces the sidewalks

from her hands escape butterflies that smell like sea.

A child catches the wind
    with his rags he builds guitars.

The doors are horizontal voids
where time languishes
and the blackberry of dreams get anesthetized.

Translated from the Spanish by Luz María López

Guatemala

Art Gatti

METRO NORTH

Southbound to NYC
I am a bullet through the trees
I am a wind through marshlands
that are *there—not there*

But in the Bronx, I am
an inevitability
I am clanking old railroad car
shock absorbers

I am a click-clack
through the projects
where cemented windows
don't deter me from being heard

I am an infernal noise
that brings expletives undeleted
an uninvited traveler through
disturbed dreams—
the slum slumber of the one who
never travels north of
the sleeplessness of despair
and broken buildings

I am metal
heading home
to vast caverns
artificially lit

"All aboard!"

New York/USA

Iliana Rodríguez Zuleta

ANNUNCIATION
In memory of my mother, Magdalena Zuleta

The room with beds, in the light.
I came in from the darkness
(the rooster crowed).
It was the announcement of her death.

Or an angel, perhaps,
one of those she loved,
haunted the room.

We kept many things silent.
Many others hurt us.
(I wouldn't want to betray her).
The rooster announces.

I'm going to miss her sometimes.
I will take care of her book and her medal.

I will also remember her hand
when we went shopping downtown
so many years ago.
She was my Tula and smiled.

Mother, walk in peace towards another light.

VISIT
To Concepción Zayas and Rosario Covarrubias, for the healing.

At the house of my friend Concepción
in Puebla,
once
there was an opossum.
A magical ancient animal.

Today his shadow is outlined
on a stone on the floor.

They tell me that last night he was
in the guest room.
He climbed into bed
or into dreams.

The truth is
that now
I feel free of pain.

Mexico

Hassanal Abdullah

THE SCATTERED DISPLAY OF LIMBS

The broken pieces of the whole world,
scattered around and laying about my feet;
I sense this horrible scene,
I sense human bloodshed—
their scratched bodies lying all around me—
walking cross human corpses,
I feel the pain of being alive.
Ah, the scattered display
of the cruel fate of my own creations
makes me impulsive—lamented and aweary.
The green that I once constructed with
both of my hands,
the road on which I mapped
everyone's desired destination,
the river I flowed from the land of my
birthplace to the pit of the ocean—
look, what the fate they have got now!
I never dreamt of this
dilapidated world,
I earnestly hoped to cross
the neighborhood and reach
the rapidly growing skyscrapers,
I fancied at the speed of an aircraft.
Every scattered piece of ruin
helplessly laying all over
is definitely a part of my limb,
how could I then walk past my own body!

I MUST WALK TOWARDS ETERNITY

Wrapped in a distant mystery,
my own past comes up and
knocks at my door. Scenes, as if
they were alive, projected on my heart's frame.
When I was exactly like you, with
the aid of my crafty little fingers,
picking out the gray hairs,
smiling, I too put a quarter or two
in my pocket—that money is now
buried beneath the shade of time.
A few of my own hairs have also grayed now.
Time toiled away even faster than that.
I know that moments of the past
would not call me again by my name.
I know those lucky quarters
would not be of any use now.
The known, intimate faces that, with the
vicious spin of time,
have gone to embrace eternity,
I sometimes
would search them in my own self.
And at the sound of your little feet,
I would also portray my past.
One day, you, too, will find your trace
in those of your children's.
And, I, turning into a gray past,
would walk towards eternity. . .
I must walk towards eternity.

Translated from Bengali by Ekok Soubir and the poet

New York/USA

58

নাজনীন সীমন

দুঃসময়ের আখ্যান

ধাইছে সময় হন্যে হয়ে
স্বপ্ন যতো সঙ্গে নিয়ে
মন জুটেছে ঘুড়ির সাথে
কে আগে আর
কে পরে যায়!

বালিশ জুড়ে কান্না-ফোঁটা
মন কেটেছে মনের বাঁধন
একলা আকাশ একলা সবাই
গভীর রাতও একলা জাগে।

পরিস্থিতির উল্টো চাপে
পর্যুদস্ত জীবন নিয়ে
কে-ই বা ভালো
থাকতে পারে
উদোম হওয়া এই প্রদেশে?

দমকা হাওয়া হঠাৎ হঠাৎ
উড়িয়ে নিলে সব আভরণ
হীরের মতো প্রকট হয়ে
দুঃখ তখন চর্তুপাশে
কিরণ ছড়ায় নিমগ্নতায়।

উন্মাদনার তুমুল সুরে
নাচছে যখন দেশ ও জাতি
সংস্কৃতিও দায় সারিয়ে
পা বাড়িয়ে উল্টা রথে
চলছে কেমন হাল্কা চালে।

ডুবছে মানুষ,
সভ্যতাও ডুবুডুবু
অসততার গভীর জলে
জাত ও বর্ণ নির্বিশেষে
সবাই এখন চোরের মাসী

খুবলে খাচ্ছে মনুষ্য নাম।

রক্ত দিয়ে সেই যে কবে
কিনেছিলো পূর্ব পুরুষ
স্বাধীনতার অমর সে গান
রক্ত চুষে মেটাচ্ছে আজ
সভ্য হবার তামাদি ঋণ।

উদোম হয়ে ঘুরছে সময়
সহবাসে তুমুল খরা
গণ্ডমূর্খ মানুষগুলো
উন্মাদনার শীর্ষ ছুঁয়ে
চিলের পেছন ছুটছে ভীষণ
বদলে দিতে দিন দুনিয়া।

মগজ ভরা দুষ্ট ক্ষত
হৃদয় জোড়া অসততা
গরম তাওয়ায় তুলছে সেঁকে
নীরব থাকা কণ্ঠস্লোগান
মন ও মনন শুকিয়ে গেছে
অসভ্যতার প্রখর রোদে।

কপাট যতো খুলবে সবই
মিথ্যেবাদীর সব আয়োজন
শেষ করাতে বিনা দ্বিধায়
জীবন জগৎ সব একাকার—
প্রতিবাদের প্রবল স্রোতে
অন্ধকার ও অত্যাচারী
সরেই যাবে নিঃসন্দেহে।

বিশ্বাসঘাতকতা

বিশ্বাসঘাতকতা করেছে সকলেই!
যাদের সর্বস্ব দিয়ে আদ্যন্ত ভালোবেসেছিলাম
ছেড়ে গেছে সবাই একের পর এক—
অনেক যত্নের পরও প্রিয় গাছেরা শুকিয়ে কাঠ হয়েছে
অথচ সার, জল, মমতার ছোঁয়া আর উজ্জ্বল সূর্যের ক্লোরেফিল
খামতি রাখিনি কোনো কিছুরই।
প্রিয় ময়না আমার, কান ফোটার সময় মরে শক্ত হয়ে থাকলো

60

অথচ সারারাত 'নীতু', 'নীতু' বলে
জাগিয়ে রেখেছিলাম যেমনটা বলেছিলো সবাই।
বিশ্বাস করে সবুজ টিয়াকে শীত দুপুরে নাতিশীতোষ্ণ জলে
স্নান করিয়ে দুপুর রোদে শুকাতে দিয়েছিলাম
কিন্তু কি আশ্চর্য, কিচ্ছু না বুঝেই
হতচ্ছাড়া ক্ষণেক সুযোগে উড়ে গেলো না বলেই;
জেনে গেলো না ওর মরিচ ছোলা ভাত ধনেপাতায়
প্রতিদিনের আদর মাখা যত্নের কাহন।
কোমায় থাকা জননীর দু'পা ছুঁয়ে বলেছিলাম ছেড়ে না যেতে
শোনেনি মা; ক্লোরিনের গন্ধমাখা হাসপাতাল থেকে বেরিয়ে বাসায় পৌঁছুতেই
চলে গেলো হুড়মুড় করে কথা না রাখার খাতায় লেখাতে নাম
যেনো শেষ ট্রেন ছেড়ে যাচ্ছে স্টেশন, প্রতিযোগিতায় নেমে পড়লো বাবাও;
বিমানের সাথে পাল্লা দিয়ে ছুটে গেলো হিমশীতল মর্গে শুয়ে থাকতে
এতো ঠাণ্ডাও হতে পারে কোনো মৃতদেহ
একে একে সবাই না বলে চলে গেলো
কি আশ্চর্য, এমনকি তুমিও . . .

কৃত্রিমতা

ঠিক চিনেছি রং মাখা মুখ তোমাদের!
পলকে বদলে যেতে পারো যখন যেমন ইচ্ছে
ঘিনঘিনে মাছির অসংখ্য চোখ ঘোরাতে ঘোরাতে বসে পড়ো
সুযোগে; আবার অন্য ঘর, তারপর . . .
দাঁড়ের উপর ক্বচিৎ, হয়তো থিতু হও খানিক
পরক্ষণেই উড়ে চলো যেনো অস্থির অশান্ত ঝড়ো হাওয়া।
ধারালো ছুরি দিয়ে টুকরো টুকরো করো বিশ্বস্ততার কবন্ধ হাড়মাংশ,
সত্য বলে দেয় এহেন শঙ্কায়
নির্দ্বিধায় নিজের ছায়াকে ফালা ফালা কেটে ফেলো এতোটাই নির্মমতায় যে
মাঘী পূর্ণিমার উজ্জ্বল রাতও খুঁজে পায় না অস্তিত্ব তার আর কখনও
বালিয়াড়িতে কঙ্কাল হয়ে পড়ে থাকে প্রিয় সময়;
অভিন্ন সত্তা বলে একদা যেমন বেঁধেছিলে মায়াবী একতারার সুর
নির্দ্বিধায় সুদীর্ঘ ভালোবাসার দৈর্ঘ্যপ্রস্থময় সেগল্প আঁস্তাকুড়ে ছুঁড়ে ফেলে
নিমেষে উল্টোরথের রশি টানতে টানতে যাও বর্ণময় নতুন কিছুর খোঁজে।
দুই পায়ে চেপে চেপে প্রবেশ করাও অতীতের মৃতদেহ খাদের গভীরে
অতঃপর ক্রমাগত এগোও আবার ভিন্ন এক দিগন্ত সন্ধানে।

নিউইয়র্ক/যুক্তরাষ্ট্র

সৌমিত্র দেব

তুমি চলে গেছো

তুমি তো চলেই গেছো, তবে কেনো বারবার ফিরে আসো সংখ্যালঘু হয়ে। গভীর রাতের পর্দা ছিঁড়ে আসো ডাকাতের বেশে। তুমুল বর্ষার কালে পাহাড়ি ঢলের সাথে বন্যা হয়ে আসো। কখনো শুনতে পাই ঘেরাও দিয়েছো তুমি সচিবালয়ের গেট। বিপন্ন আনসার হয়ে তুলে ধরো বেদনার মহাকাব্যখানি। অথবা রিকশাওয়ালা, শ্রমজীবী নিরন্ন মানুষ। তুমি তো আইনের লোক, পুলিশের মাঝে দেখি তোমার চেহারা। তুমি কি শিশির বিন্দু লাল রং সবুজ ঘাসের?

ঢাকা/বাংলাদেশ

সৌরভ সিকদার

কবির বাড়ি

প্রথমে যে ঘরটায় ঢুকবেন সেখানে বৃক্ষরা
পিটি করার জন্য
দাঁড়িয়ে আছে সারি সারি সবুজ পোষাক পরে
ডানদিক থেকে দলপতি বেলি ফুলের সুগন্ধ দিয়ে
অভিবাদন জানাবে আপনাকে
কেমন যেন স্নিগ্ধতায় ভরে যাবে উড়ু উড়ু মন,
সবুজের এই চিড়িয়াখানায় বড় বেমানান ট্রেডমিলটিও
জানিয়ে দিচ্ছে গাছেদের এখন দৌড়বার সময়
মানুষের মতো ওরাও কোলস্টেরল আর সুগারকে
বেড়ো ভয় পায়,
এরপর যে ঘরটিতে আপনি প্রবেশ করবেন
সেটা একটা জীবন্ত লাইব্রেরি, সারি সারি বইয়ের
তাক থেকে বেরিয়ে আপনাকে স্বাগত জানাবে
শামসুর রাহমান, হুমায়ুন আজাদ আর
আবুল হাসান দেয়ালে টাঙানো
অনেক ফ্রেম থেকে
বঙ্গবন্ধু বেরিয়ে এসে বলবেন, এবারের সংগ্রাম
আমাদের মুক্তির সংগ্রাম,
বৈঠকটেবিলে পুরাতন বই, চিঠি আর বাংলা
লিটিলম্যাগাজিনগুলো বড়ো গাদাগাদি
করে শুয়ে আছে
তাদের মাঝ থেকে হঠাৎ দাঁড়িয়ে
আপনার সাথে করমর্দন করবে
কপালে ভাঁজ পড়া শব্দশৈলী
এরপর আপনি যে কক্ষে প্রবেশ করবেন
সেটা কবির প্রার্থনার টেবিল,
সেখানে একটি সোনালি কলম আপনাকে
দেখে নড়েচড়ে বসবে
কবির ভাবনাভার বয়ে বয়ে
সে এখন কিছুটা ক্লান্ত
তার নাকের ডগায়
বিন্দু বিন্দু ঘাম থেকে ঝরে পড়বে অজস্র
দ্যোতনাময় শব্দ আর আপনি অভিভূত হয়ে

63

Shabdaguchha

তাকিয়ে দেখবেন দরোজার পাশে
দাঁড়িয়ে আছেন কবির স্ত্রী
তাঁর হাতে ধোঁয়া ওঠা কাপ
আপনাকে শোনাবে অনাগত দিনের সবচেয়ে
আকর্ষণীয় কোনো কবিতা!
এই হচ্ছে কবির বাড়ি,
এখানে কবিতা ও প্রকৃতি একটেবিলে
কফি খেতে খেতে চায়ের জন্য দীর্ঘশ্বাস ফেলে!

ঢাকা/বাংলাদেশ

তারেক মাহমুদ

ধবধবে সাদা রাত

বনানীর ১৮ নম্বর সড়ক দিয়ে হাঁটছিলাম রাতে
নিয়নবাতির রূপসী আলোর রাস্তায়
দীঘল খোলাচুলে সাদা শাড়ি পরা
অসাধারণ এক অচেনা ঝলমলে তরুণী
মুখরিত হাসি দিয়ে আমার পাশে দাঁড়ালো
বললো—যাবে?
বললাম—কোথায়?
বললো—সামনেই এক উচ্চবিত্ত কবরস্থান আছে। যাবে?
বললাম—নিশ্চয়ই। কবরস্থান আমার খুব প্রিয়। জীবনের মানে খুঁজে পাই।
সাদা শাড়ি পরা তরুণীটি আমার হাত ধরলো
আমরা এগিয়ে যেতে থাকলাম কবরস্থানের দিকে . . .

০৮. ১০. ২০২৩
ঢাকা/বাংলাদেশ

ধী শংকর

অক্ষত

সেই যে আমাদের প্রাঙ্গণ ভেঙে
একটা নতুন বিল্ডিং তুলতে শুরু করেছিলো
মনে আছে তোর?
আজ দেখি সেটা তৈরি হয়ে গেছে। সুন্দর মার্বেলের সিঁড়ি বেয়ে
অনেক উঁচুতে উঠে পড়েছি আমি।
রোদে দাঁড়িয়ে আছি, কষ্ট পাবার জন্য।
অনেক কষ্ট করে কষ্ট পেতে হয় আজকাল,
আগের মতো সহজে আর পারি না।
মনে আছে মেয়ে, সেই যে তুই
ক্যাম্পাসের পাশের একটা মাধবীলতানো বাড়ির দিকে তাকিয়ে
বলতিস, "আমাকে ওই বাড়িটায় থাকতে দেয় না কেনো?"
এই নতুন বিল্ডিংয়ের তিনতলা থেকে
সেই বাড়িটাকে কতো ভালো করে দেখা যাচ্ছে।
দেখতে পাচ্ছিস?
যদি জানতিস, দেখতে ইচ্ছে করতো?

আবার যখন কলকাতায় আসবি, বাড়ি আসবি, দেখে যাস।
আশপাশের বাড়িগুলো কি পুরোনো, গলিগুলো কি গরিব।
সব খুব ভালো করে দেখা যাচ্ছে।

মহীনের কনসার্টের দিন ঠিক কোনখানটায় দাঁড়িয়েছিলাম বল তো?
এই বিল্ডিংটা কি সে জায়গাটা ঢেকে দিয়েছে?
আমাদের কষ্ট আর আন্দোলন দেখ কেমন মার্বেলে বাঁধা পড়েছে।
এখন আমরা খুশি।
তোর কথা খুব মনে পড়ছে। নোনতা স্বাদ নামছে ঠোঁটে।

বিল্ডিংটা বড্ড নতুন। বাড়িটা পুরোনো। কথা দে আসবি না?

কলকাতা/ভারত

শব্দ সংবাদ / SHABDA NEWS

ন্যাম কবিতা পুরস্কার পেলেন কবি হাসানআল আব্দুল্লাহ

২২তম ন্যাম আন্তর্জাতিক কবিতা পুরস্কার পেলেন কবি ও শব্দগুচ্ছ সম্পাদক হাসানআল আব্দুল্লাহ। লেবাননে অবস্থিত ন্যাম ফাউন্ডেশনের হেডকোয়ার্টার থেকে জুলাইয়ের প্রথম সপ্তাহে এই পুরস্কার ঘোষণা করা হয়। মোট চারটি শাখায় বিশ্বের নানা দেশের কবিদের এই পুরস্কার দেয়া হয়। হাসানআল আব্দুল্লাহ পুরস্কারটি পেয়েছেন ক্রিয়েটিভ শাখায়। এর আগে এ বছর জানুয়ারি মাসে কবিকে এই পুরস্কারের জন্যে নমিনেশন দেন পোলিশ রাইটার্স ইউনিয়নের প্রেসিডেন্ট। উল্লেখ্য কবি হাসানআল আব্দুল্লাহ ইতিপূর্বে আরো দুটি আন্তর্জাতিক পুরস্কারে ভূষিত হয়েছেন। ২০১৬ সালে পেয়েছেন হোমার ইয়োরোপিয় কবিতা পুরস্কার ও ২০২১ সালে পেয়েছেন ক্লেমেন্স জেনেঙ্কি কবিতা পুরস্কার। তাছাড়া তিনি নিউইয়র্ক কালচারাল এফেয়ার্স থেকে পেয়েছেন অনুবাদ গ্রান্ট (২০১৯), নতুন ধারার স্বতন্ত্র সনেটের জন্যে লেবুভাই ফাউন্ডেশন পুরস্কার (২০১৩), পুশকার্ট নমিনেশন ও ২০০৭ সালে তিনি কুইন্স পোয়ে পোয়েট লরিয়েট ফাইনালিস্ট-এর গৌরব অর্জন করেন। সাহিত্যের নানা শাখায় কবি হাসানআল আব্দুল্লাহর প্রকাশিত গ্রন্থসংখ্যা পঞ্চাশের অধিক। অনন্যা প্রকাশনি থেকে দুইখণ্ডে প্রকাশ পেয়েছে তাঁর 'কবিতাসমগ্র'। দেশের একাধিক বিশ্ববিদ্যালয়ে পড়ানো হয় তাঁর বই 'কবিতার ছন্দ' (বাংলা একাডেমি)। তিনি সম্পাদনা করেছেন 'বিশশতকের বাংলা কবিতা' (মাওলা), ও 'ওয়ার্ল্ড পোয়েট্রি অ্যান্থোলজি' (ডার্কলাইট পাবলিশিং)। অনুবাদ করেছেন 'কনটেম্পোরারি বাংলাদেশি পোয়েট্রি' (ফেরল প্রেস)। তাঁর কবিতা অনূদিত হয়েছে পনেরোটি ভাষায়, স্থান পেয়েছে আঠারোটি আন্তর্জাতিক এন্থোলজিতে। তাঁর গ্রন্থ 'আন্ডার দ্যা থিন লেয়ারস অব লাইট' ইংরেজি, চাইনিজ, পোলিশ ও স্প্যানিশ ভাষায় অনূদিত হয়ে যথাক্রমে যুক্তরাষ্ট্র, তাইওয়ান, পোল্যান্ড ও মেক্সিকো থেকে প্রকাশ পেয়েছে। তিনি আমন্ত্রিত কবি হিসেবে যোগ দিয়েছেন চীন, গ্রীস, পোল্যান্ড, ভারত, কানাডা, মেক্সিকো, কেনিয়া ও মরক্কোতে অনুষ্ঠিত আন্তর্জাতিক কবিতা উৎসবে। যুক্তরাষ্ট্রের লাইব্রেরি অব কংগ্রেসে এ পর্যন্ত স্থান পেয়েছে তাঁর লিখিত ২৭টি গ্রন্থ। হাসানআল আব্দুল্লাহ 'শব্দগুচ্ছ' কবিতাপত্রিকা সম্পাদক ও নিউইয়র্ক সিটি হাইস্কুলের গণিত ও কম্পিউটার বিষয়ে সিনিয়র শিক্ষক।

'শব্দগুচ্ছ' পুরস্কার পেলেন পোলিশ কবি কাজিমেয়ারেজ বুরনাত

'শব্দগুচ্ছ' আন্তর্জাতিক কবিতা পুরস্কার ২০২৩ পেলেন কবি কাজিমেয়ারেজ বুরনাত। ১৬ ডিসেম্বর সন্ধ্যায় শব্দগুচ্ছ অফিসে এক কবিতা পাঠের অনুষ্ঠানে এ পুরস্কার ঘোষণা করেন সম্পাদক কবি হাসানআল আব্দুল্লাহ। অনুষ্ঠানে স্থানীয় কবি, সাহিত্যিক ও সাংবাদিকগণ উপস্থিত ছিলেন। কাজিমেয়ারেজ বুরনাত একজন পোলিশ কবি এবং ভ্রসলোভ শহরে অবস্থিত পোলিশ রাইটার্স

ইউনিয়নের নিম্ন সাইলেসিয়ান শাখার সভাপতি। তিনি এই পুরস্কার পেয়েছেন "বিশ্ব কবিতায় তাঁর উল্লেখযোগ্য অবদানের জন্য।" তাঁর কবিতা ৪৩টি ভাষাটায় অনূদিত হয়েছে। তিনি পুরস্কারের সম্মানী পাবেন পাঁচশত ডলার ও একটি ক্রেস্ট। এ বছর জুরি বোর্ডের সদস্য ছিলেন নিউইয়র্ক বিশ্ববিদ্যালয়ের ইংরেজি সাহিত্যের অধ্যাপক নিকোলসন বার্নস, কবি বিল ওয়ালেক, কবি ও শিক্ষাবিদ নাজনীন সীমন এবং কবি হাসানআল আবদুল্লাহ (সমন্বয়ক)। বিজয় দিবস ও পুরস্কার ঘোষণা উপলক্ষে আয়োজিত এই অনুষ্ঠানে বিভিন্ন পর্যায়ে কবিতাপাঠ ও আলোচনায় অংশ নেন কবি ও মুক্তিযোদ্ধা ফারুক আজম, ঠিকানা পত্রিকার প্রধান সম্পাদক ফজলুর রহমান, কবি আল ইমরান সিদ্দিকী, শিল্পী মিনি কাদির, প্রফেসর হুসনে আরা, বিশিষ্ট সংগঠক নাজমুল কাদির, 'বাঙালী' পত্রিকার সাংবাদিক আসলাম আহমেদ খান, কবি ও শিক্ষাবিদ নাজনীন সীমন, শিক্ষিকা মনিরা আকঞ্জি, ও মাহমুদা খাতুন রেখা। অনুষ্ঠানে আরো উপস্থিত ছিলেন শিল্পী সুব্রত দত্ত, নিরুপমা দত্ত ও নতুন প্রজন্মের একঝাঁক বাঙালী শিক্ষার্থীরা। বক্তাদের আলোচনায় বিজয় দিবসের মাহাত্ম্য, মুক্তিযুদ্ধের অভিজ্ঞতা, তিরিশ লক্ষ শহীদ, ও পৃথিবীর দেশে দেশে যুদ্ধ-বৈষম্য এবং এ থেকে উত্তরের নানা কৌশল ও পরামর্শ স্থান পায়। কবি হাসানআল আব্দুল্লাহ 'শব্দগুচ্ছ পুরস্কার' ঘোষণার আগে গত ২৫ বছরের এই পত্রিকার মাধ্যমে যে আন্তর্জাতিক প্লাটফর্ম তৈরি হয়েছে তার নাতিদীর্ঘ পরিচিতি তুলে ধরে বলেন যে বিশ্বের নানা দেশের কবিদের সাথে সেতুবন্ধন তৈরি করাই এই পত্রিকার প্রধান লক্ষ্য। উল্লেখ্য শব্দগুচ্ছ কবিতা পুরস্কার প্রবর্তিত হয় ২০০১ সালে। তখন থেকে প্রতি দু'বছর পরপর এই পত্রিকার লেখকদের ভেতর থেকে একজনকে এই সম্মান দেয়া হয়।

চলে গেলেন মার্কিন কবি স্ট্যানলি মস

শুক্রবার, ৫ জুলাই, চলে গেলেন মার্কিন কবি ও প্রকাশক স্ট্যানলি মস। মৃত্যুকালে তাঁর বয়স হয়েছিলো ৯৯ বছর। তিনি ১৯২৫ সালে কুইন্স কাউন্টির উডেহেভেন শহরে জন্ম গ্রহন করেন। তিনি ১৬টি গ্রন্থের প্রণেতা। ১৯৭৭ সালে তিনি শিল্প মোডো প্রেস নামে একটি প্রকাশনা সংস্থা শুরু করেন। বিখ্যাত কবি ডিলান টমাস ও স্ট্যানলি কিউনিটজ-এর সাথে তাঁর বিশেষ বন্ধুতা গড়ে ওঠে। পরে, আর্ট ডিলার হিসেবে ল্যুভর ও মেট্রোপলিটন ইত্যাদি মিউজিয়ামে বিশেষত ইটালিয়ান আর্ট বিক্রি করে তিনি বিত্তশালী হন। 'শব্দগুচ্ছ' (Shabdaguchha) বিভিন্ন সময়ে তাঁর কবিতা প্রকাশ করেছে এবং 'শব্দগুচ্ছ' সম্পাদকের সাথে এই কবির বিশেষ হৃদ্যতা হয়। তাঁর মৃত্যুতে 'শব্দগুচ্ছ' পরিবার গভীরভাবে শোকাহত।

I paint good news on a krater, neither fake;
the word poetry comes from the Greek to make,
the Chinese character is to keep.
A rattlesnake, I want to make and keep.
(*from 'Murder', Stanley Moss, Shabdaguchha, Issue 82/83, 2021*)

তারেক মাহমুদের বিদায়

কবি, সম্পাদক, অভিনেতা ও নির্মাতা তারেক মাহমুদ চলে গেলেন। বেশ কয়েক বছর ধরেই তিনি একপ্রকার নির্বাসিত জীবন যাপন করছিলেন। মৃত্যুর দু'দিন আগেই তিনি লেখেন, "ভুল মানুষের কাছে তোমার মনটা বিনিয়োগ করো না। যদি করো হয়তো তুমি তোমাকেই হারিয়ে ফেলবে।" অথচ, সব কষ্ট বুকে চেপেও দিনের পর দিন তাঁকে হাসি-খুশি থাকতে দেখা গেছে। তিনি বলছিলেন, "আমি প্রচণ্ডভাবে আমার শৈশব দ্বারা তাড়িত, যৌবন দ্বারা নয়। আর তাই বড়ো হওয়া হলো না আমার। বয়সী শিশু হয়ে থাকাটাই আমার আনন্দ।" অথচ, এভাবে বলার বাইরেও কী তীব্র কষ্ট বুকের ভেতর লালন করে চলেছিলেন তারেক! যা হয়তো তাঁর ঘনিষ্ঠজনেরা কখনও বুঝতে পারেননি।

বড্ড অভিমানেই বোধহয় তারেক বলেছিলেন, "৩০ বছরের ঢাকায় বসবাসের জীবনে এমন একজন কাছের মানুষ হলো না আমার, যে নিজের মন থেকে জানতে চাইবে 'তারেক কেমন আছো? ঠিকঠাক আছো তো? খারাপ লাগলে কল দিও। কিছু প্রয়োজন হলে অবশ্যই জানাবে কিন্তু। ভালো থেকো।' সত্যিই নেই। দেখা হলে অনেকেই আপন। তারপর আর কেউ নেই। যদি কিছু পেতে হয় তবে চেয়ে চেয়ে নিতে হয়। তবুও এই শহরটাকে ভালোবাসি।" কবিতা যাপন নিয়ে তিনি বলেছিলেন, "কবিতাকে আমি অক্সিজেনের সঙ্গে তুলনা করতে চাই। আসলে লেখাটাই আমার একমাত্র নিজস্ব কাজ। আত্মার আঙারা ছাড়া কি লেখা যায়?"

অভিনয় তাঁর পেশা হলেও লেখালেখি ও লিটলম্যাগ আন্দোলন ছিলো তাঁর নেশা। ১৯৯৭ সাল থেকে তিনি ছোটকাগজ 'পথিক' সম্পাদনা করেছেন। কখনও নিয়মিত, কখনও বা অনিয়মিত। তাঁর জন্ম পাবনায়। লেখালেখি, সম্পাদনা ও অভিনয়ের কারণে ঢাকায় অবস্থান করছেন প্রায় ত্রিশ বছর। 'পাবনার কবি ও কবিতা' গ্রন্থের জন্য নেয়া সাক্ষাৎকার থেকে জানা যায় তারেক মাহমুদের প্রথম কবিতাগ্রন্থ 'কালের বাঁশি' প্রকাশিত হয়েছিল ১৯৯৭ সালে। এরপর নির্দিষ্ট বিরতিতে প্রকাশিত হয়েছে যথাক্রমে 'ফিরে যাচ্ছি হ্রদের কাছে', 'মেঘেরা ডেকেছিলো, যাইনি', 'সুবর্ণার চোখ', 'ভালোবাসা কথাটি যেভাবে বলা দরকার', 'আকাশ বলে কিছু নেই', 'প্রিপেইড ভালোবাসা', 'সখি আমি তোমার সখাই আছি', 'তোমাকে ভুলে গেছি মনে রাখতে গিয়ে', 'পেরিয়ে যাচ্ছি সকল দরজা', 'কাতার সোজা করে দাঁড়ান' ও 'কুড়ি বছরের কবিতা'। তাঁর লেখা অন্যান্য বইগুলোর মধ্যে উপন্যাস: 'সুমিতার জন্য', 'ডোরা', 'তোমার সাথে কিছু কথা ছিলো'; গল্পগ্রন্থ: 'জলযোগ রেস্তোরাঁ'; আত্মজীবনীমূলক গ্রন্থ: 'বালকবেলা'; ও চলচ্চিত্র বিষয়ক বই: 'ইসমাইল মোহাম্মদ উদয়ন চৌধুরী চলচ্চিত্র ও অন্যান্য প্রসঙ্গ' উল্লেখযোগ্য। তারেক মাহমুদ নির্মিত পূর্ণদৈর্ঘ্য চলচ্চিত্র 'চটপটি' রিলিজের প্রতিক্ষায় ছিলো।

সম্পাদকের জার্নাল / EDITOR'S JOURNAL

নিউইয়র্ক কবিতা উৎসব ও বইমেলা

দুই দিনের নিউইয়র্ক কবিতা উৎসব ও বইমেলার আজ (১৩ জুন, ২০২৪) ছিলো প্রথম দিন। আমি বসেছিলাম আমার প্রকাশক ডার্কলাইট পালিশিং-এর স্টলে। আর আমার সঙ্গী হয়েছিলেন ঢাকা থেকে আগত আরেক প্রকাশক লানন্দা'র স্বত্বাধিকারী জুয়েল রেদওয়ান। আমি মঞ্চে কবিতা পড়ার আগে আমার দুই প্রকাশককে ধন্যবাদ জানালাম। রবার্টো কবিতা পড়লেন আমার আগে। সারাদিন কতো কতো কবিদের সাথে দেখা ও আলাপ হলো।বেশ ভালো একটা কবিতাময় দিন গেলো। মারিয়া লিসেলা ও আমি ছিলাম ২০০৭ সালের কুইন্স পোয়েট লরিয়ট ফাইনালস্ট। মারিয়া পরে পোয়েট লরিয়েট হন, কিন্তু গত দশ বছরেও সেই পদে কোনো পরিবর্তন আসেনি। তিনি বললেন, তিনি এ নিয়ে পত্রিকায় আর্টিকেল লিখেছেন। তার একটা কপি দিয়ে বললেন, টাইটেলটা তোমার হোক সেটা আমি চাই। আমি বলি, তুমি চাইলেই তো হবে না। কমিটি সিদ্ধান্ত নেবে।তিনি বললেন, তারা কি করছে কে জানে! কিছুক্ষণ পরে তিনি নিউজার্সির কবি মেঘাকে নিয়ে এলেন। পরিচয় করিয়ে দিয়ে তিনি বললেন, হাসানআল-এর অনেক পাবলিকেশন্স, আন্তর্জাতিক অঙ্গনে বিচরণ, পত্রিকা সম্পাদনা ইত্যাদি দিয়ে ব্যস্ত সময় পার হয়। আমার নামের সাথে চমৎকার একটা বিশেষণ তিনি যোগ করলে আমি হো হো করে হাসলাম। মেঘা আমার দুটো বই কিনলেন। একজন তরুণ আফ্রিকান-আমেরিকান কবি 'কনটেম্পোরারি বাংলাদেশি পোয়েট্রি' কিনে বললেন, ভবিষ্যতে আমি আরো বাংলাদেশের কবিতা সংগ্রহ করবো। এলেন মিন্ডি ক্রোনেনবার্গ! ২০০০ সালে তিনি আমার প্রথম বাইলিঙ্গুয়াল বইয়ের দারুণ একটা রিভিউ লিখেছিলেন। ক্রস ওয়েবারকে দেখে রীতিমতো অবাক হলাম, বয়সের ছাপ ভীষণভাবে ধরা পড়েছে। তাঁর সঙ্গী ক্রসকে জিজ্ঞেস করলেন, তুমি আগে থেকে হাসানআলকে চিনতে। ক্রস মাথা নাড়লেন। আমি বললাম, শতাব্দীর শুরুতে আমরা কবিতা নিয়ে একসাথে কাজ করেছি। তবে, কেনো বাদ দিয়েছিলাম সেটা বলিনি। টম বললেন, এক কবি তাকে ইটালিয়ান কয়েকজন কবিকে অনুবাদ করে দিতে বলেছেন তার পত্রিকার জন্যে। আমি কবির নাম শুনে বললাম, একটু সাবধানে, বাংলাদেশের দশজন কবির কবিতা তাকে একবার দিয়েও আমি ফেরত নিয়েছিলাম, কারণ তিনি অপমানজনকভাবে প্রচ্ছদে আমাদের প্লেস করেছিলেন। আমাদের স্বাধীনতা সংগ্রামের ইতিহাস তুলে ধরে বললাম, আমার দেশের কবিদের ছোটো করার কোনো সুযোগ আমি কাউকে দেবো না। তিনি বললেন, আমি তোমাকে এ জন্যে সম্মান প্রদর্শন করছি। মেলার শেষ দিকে এলেন বিল ওয়ালেক। কিছুক্ষণ আমাদের সাথে বসলেন। এরপর কবিতা পড়তে গেলেন। মেলার চারপাশে চারটি মঞ্চ থেকে সারা দিন লাগাতার কবিতা পাঠ হলো।

২.
আমি আমার প্রকাশকের স্টলে বই বিক্রিতে সাহায্য করছিলাম। ঘটনাটি নিউইয়র্ক সিটি কবিতা উৎসবের প্রথম দিনের। আমার সামনে দাঁড়ানো এই তরুণ কবি, আমার

অনূদিত 'কনটেম্পোরারি বাংলাদেশী পোয়েট্রি' সংগ্রহ করে বললেন, "আমার বইয়ের তাকে বাংলা কবিতার এটাই প্রথম বই। তবে আমি অচিরেই আরো বই সংগ্রহ করবো।" আমি খুশি হয়ে তাকে ধন্যবাদ জানালাম। দ্বিতীয় দিন ক্যালিফোর্নিয়া থেকে আসা আরেক কবি হন্তদন্ত হয়ে বইটা তুলে নিয়ে বললেন, "আমি আরেকটা স্টলে কাজ করছি, সময় কম, একটু ছুটি নিয়ে এসেছি বইটা সংগ্রহ করতে। আমাকে দুটি কপি দিন একটা আমার আরেকটা আমার বন্ধুর জন্য।' তিনি জানালেন তাঁর বন্ধু বলেছেন বইটা বেশ ভালো। এবারও আমি খুশি হয়ে তাঁকে ধন্যবাদ জানালাম। মেলা থেকে আমার বিভিন্ন বইয়ের ১৬টি কপি বিক্রি হয়েছে। আমি যারপরনাই কৃতজ্ঞ!

১. কনটেম্পোরারে বাংলাদেশি পোয়েট্রি/৪খানা
২. ওয়ার্ল্ড পোয়েট্রি এন্থোলজি/৫খানা
৩. আন্ডার দ্য থিন লেয়ারস অব লাইট/১খানা
৪. টেনশন ইন এনট্যাঙ্গেলড কাইটস/১খানা
৫. দ্যা ব্যাক সাইড/১খানা
৬. 'শব্দগুচ্ছ' (২৫ বর্ষপূর্তি সংখ্যা)/৩খানা
৭. 'শব্দগুচ্ছ' (পোলিশ সংখ্যা)/১খানা

তাছাড়া বেশ কয়েকজন কবিকে 'শব্দগুচ্ছ' সৌজন্য কপি ও একজন কবিকে 'ওয়ার্ল্ড পোয়েট্রি এন্থোলজি' প্রকাশকের পক্ষ থেকে রিভিউ কপি দেয়া হয়েছে। মেলার প্রথম দিন কবি ও সংগঠক গর্ডন গিলবার্টের আমন্ত্রণে 'দ্য পোয়েট্রি টেবল'- এর ব্যানারে ফিচার হিসেবে কবিতা পড়েছি।

শিক্ষকতার সাতাশ বছর

এই শহরে আমার প্রথম কাজটি ছিলো অত্যন্ত কঠিন, সপ্তাহে ৫৪ ঘন্টা! সেটা সেই ১৯৯০ সালের কথা। এর পরের কাজটি একটু হালকা, তবে তখন ৭২ ঘণ্টা কাজ করতাম। এর পরের বছর থেকে কলেজে যাওয়া শুরু করলাম, ততোদিনে ঢাকা বিশ্ববিদ্যালয়ের ট্রান্সক্রিপ্ট চলে এসেছিলো। দিনে কলেজে যেতাম, রাতে কাজ করতাম, উপরন্তু শনিবারে বারো ঘণ্টা, আর রবিবারে ১৮ ঘণ্টা। ১৯৯৫ সালে কলেজ গ্রাজুয়েশনের পর চাকরির অফার, পিএইচডি করার সুযোগ বাদ দিয়েও কিছুদিন অন্যকাজ (অড-জব) করেছি শিক্ষকতায় থাকবো বলে, কারণ কবিতা লেখাটা চালিয়ে যেতে চেয়েছিলাম মনেপ্রাণে। মডেল হিসেবে ছিলেন জীবনানন্দ দাশ ও বুদ্ধদেব বসু। ১৯৯৭ সালে এক বছর শিক্ষকতা করেছি লাগুর্ডিয়া কমিউনিটি কলেজে। পরের বছর থেকে হাইস্কুলে ফুলটাইম শিক্ষক। শিক্ষকতার পাশাপাশি মাঝে তিন বছর ছিলাম এসএলসি ডিরেক্টর, চার বছর ডাটা এনালিস্ট ও শেষ পাঁচ বছর ম্যাথ ডিপার্টমেন্ট চেয়ার। আমার ২৭ বছরের শিক্ষকতা জীবনের শেষ দিন ছিলো ২৬ জুন, ২০২৪! কতো কতো ছাত্রছাত্রী, শিক্ষক ও অভিভাবকের ভালবাসা, সম্মান পেয়েছি। ভাবতেই পারছি না এতোগুলো বছর পার হয়ে গেলো! স্মৃতির খাতায় জমা হয়ে থাকলো কতো কতো মহার্ঘ সময়!

LETTERS TO THE EDITOR:

1.
Hassanal,

All the best. Many thanks for the 25th anniversary issue of *Shabdaguchha*. It got to me even though you had my old address . . . I've been reading the issue with pleasure (many very strong poems from the community you've supported . . . Sorry I'm not in it . . . from the Woodhaven of my earliest childhood. You are a poetry light on our globe . . . Hope you and your loved ones are well these tiring days. Thanks again.

William Heyen
Brockport, New York
September 10, 2023

2.
Dear Hassanal,

Auguri as we say in Italian . . . you have outdone yourself . . . Poets from 25 countries . . . amazing the range, the nuanced differences in sensibilities . . . it was like traveling the world.

I read cover to cover your 25th Anniversary issue ... so many good pieces ...I have many page corners turned down in order to bring me back to favorites . . .

Thank you for the issue.

Maria Lisella
Queens Poet Laureate
August 15, 2024

Contributors:

Hassanal Abdullah is an author of more than 50 books in various genres including 20 collections of poetry, and the editor of *Shabdaguchha*, an international bilingual poetry magazine. His *Collected Poems* (in Bengali) was published by Ananya in two Volumes. Mr. Abdullah received the Homer European Medal of Poetry and Art (2016), Klement Janesky International Poetry Award (2021) from Poland, and a translation Grant from New York City Department of Cultural Affairs (2019). His poetry has been translated into fifteen languages and was published in various poetry anthologies throughout the world. He introduced *Swatantra Sonnets*, seven-seven stanza pattern and abcdabc efgdefg rhyming scheme, and wrote an epic illustrating the human relationships with cosmology. As an invited guest, he attended international poetry festivals in China, Poland, Greece, Kenya, Morocco, Mexico, Canada, and India. Mr. Abdullah teaches math.

Bengt Berg, lives and works in Värmland, western Sweden. He has published more than 40 books, mostly poetry and often in collaboration with various artists or with his own photographic images. Since the poet lives in the forest and lake landscape, nature and landscape also play an important role in his poetry. Added to this are the impressions from his many journeys around the world: India, Bangladesh, China, Vietnam, Latin America and many European countries. Bengt Berg's poems have been translated into many languages and he has participated in many poetry festivals around the world.

Bengt O Björklund is a poet, journalist, photographer, musician, writer, and artist. He was born in Stockholm in 1949. In 1968, he landed in prison in Istanbul where he met a bunch of international artists, poets and musicians. It was there he began his creative activity. In 2018, Bengt was named Sweden Beat Poet Laureate and honored with a lifetime award by the National Beat Poetry Foundation, Inc. based in Connecticut, USA. He is the author of five poetry collections in Swedish and two in English. He lives in Stockholm with his artist wife, Gertrude.

Svitlana Breslavska is a Ukrainian writer, translator, literary critic, and compiler of anthologies and almanacs. She is a member of the National Union of Writers of Ukraine, the Writers' Union of Poland, and the Society of Literary Translators. Her works include 6 books of poetry, 2 books of short stories, and 17 books of translations from Polish into Ukrainian. She is the first translator of Witkacy's works into Ukrainian. She has participated in international festivals and conferences.

Kazimierz Burnat is a Polish poet, translator, publicist, journalist, and an animator of the literary movement. His poems have been translated into many languages, including English, Ukrainian, Vietnamese, Chinese, Mongolian, Swedish, Serbian, and Latvian. He is the president of the Polish Writers' Union and the host of an annual International Poetry Festival in Polanica-Zdrój. He published eight books of poetry and co-authored about one hundred and eighty anthologies, almanacs and monographs published in Poland and abroad.

John Burroughs of Cleveland is a dog-loving traveling writer who served as the 2022-2023 U.S. National Beat Poet Laureate and previously served as Ohio's Beat Poet Laureate. Burroughs is the author of *The Wrest of the Worthwhile* (Far Queue Press,

2023), *Rattle & Numb* (Venetian Spider Press, 2019) and around twenty poetry chapbooks. He currently serves as a vice president for the Ohio Poetry Association and since 2008 has been the founding editor and publisher for Crisis Chronicles Press.

Manfred Chobot is an Austrian poet who was born in Vienna. He is the Member of the Austrian Writers League, the Austrian Authors Association, the International Authors Association, *Kogge,* and the co-founder of the First Vienna Theatre of Reading Performances. Apart from Bening a writer, Chobot is the editor of the series of books, *Lyrik aus Osterreich* (Poetry from Austria), and the editorial staff of the literary magazine, *Podium.* He has held Exhibitions of *Bild Gedichte* and set approximately fifty radio plays for various broadcasting stations. He is the author of twelve poetry collections, twenty-six collections of prose, two novels, two volumes of photo books, and two books of children in German. His poetry has been translated into many languages.

Soumitra Dev is the editor of *redtimesbd.com*, an online news portal. A poet, journalist, and social activist, he is the author of more than twenty books in different genres. He received the Mother Theresa Gold Medal in Philanthropy (2023) from Mina Foundation, Dhaka. Mr. Dev lives in Dhaka with his family.

Joan Digby is Professor Emeritus of English Literature and former Director of the Poetry Center—at Long Island University. She and her late husband, British poet and collagist, John Digby, co-founded The Feral Press, a small press publishing limited editions primarily of poetry. Their more than 350 publications are collected by many university libraries. A past-presidents of the National Collegiate Honors Council, Joan has published academic work on higher education in addition to several books of poetry. Much of her work is focused on the human connection to animals, both fictional and real.

Sara Ehsan is a poet and playwright. Born in Iran, she came to Germany as a refugee at the age of eight. While studying literature, Iranian studies and art history in Heidelberg, she began publishing her texts in magazines, newspapers and anthologies. Publication of four volumes of poetry: 2011 *Deutschland Mon Amour* (Germany Mon Amour), 2020 *Bestimmung / Calling*, 2022 *Un-Liebesgedichte & Un- Love Poems*, 2023 *das flüstern der anderen* (the whispering of the others). 2021 Participation in the International Poetry Festival Jönköping, Sweden and receipt of an artist grant from the Ministry of Science, Research and the Arts Baden-Württemberg for her book *das flüstern der anderen.*

Fatemeh Ekhtesari is an Iranian poet. She has lived in Karaj and she writes in Persian. In 2013, she appeared at the poetry festival in Gothenburg (*Göteborgs poesifestival*). After she arrived back in Iran she was imprisoned and later released on bail. Her verdict came in 2015 when she was sentenced to 99 lashes and 11.5 years imprisonment for crimes against the Iranian government, for immoral behavior and blasphemy. She now lives in Norway.

Art Gatti's pogo-stick poetic career began in '65, when he won C.U.N.Y.'s top manuscript of poetry award, then corresponded with poet Robert Bly. After decades in journalism and as a celebrated chef, he returned to poetry earth in 2000. He now translates bilingual poetry. In print, he offers us *Songs of Mute Eagles* and *Mexico, Dust in My Blood.* His poems are in dozens of print and online poetry magazines.

Sankha Ghosh (1932 – 2021) was an Indian poet and literary critic who wrote in Bengali. He was born in Chandpur District, Bangladesh. Ghosh taught at many educational institutions, including Bangabasi College, City College (all affiliated to the University of Calcutta) and at Jadavpur University, Jangipur College, Berhampore Girls' College all in Kolkata and West Bengal. He retired from Jadavpur University in 1992. In 1967, he participated in the International Writing Program's Fall Residency at the University of Iowa in Iowa City. He also taught at Delhi University, the Indian Institute of Advanced Studies at Shimla, and at the Visva-Bharati University. He won many awards including Jnanpith in 2016 from the Govt of India.

Laura Gravaglia is an Italian poet, journalist, teacher and the founder and president of La Casa della Poesia di Como (www.lacasadellapoesiadicomo.com). She is the director of the International Poetry Festival "Europa in Versi" that takes place every year in Como. Her poetry has been translated into many languages and she has attended numerous International Poetry festivals around the world.

Joan Harrison is a Professor Emerita of Long Island University-Post, where she taught art and photography for many years. Her work is included in many publications as well as in public and private collections including those of the Morgan Library in NYC, Bryn Mar College in Pennsylvania and ArtPool in Hungary. In addition to making pastels, paintings, photographs and collages, Arcadia Press published three visual histories of Glen Cove that she authored as well as a co-written one on Locust Valley, Long Island, NY.

William Heyen was born in Brooklyn, New York. He is Professor of English/Poet in Residence Emeritus at SUNY Brockport. His MA and Ph.D. degrees are from Ohio University. A former Senior Fulbright Lecturer in American Literature in Germany, he has won NEA, Guggenheim, American Academy & Institute of Arts & Letters, and other fellowships and awards. He is the editor of American Poets in 1976, The Generation of 2000: Contemporary American Poets, and September 11, 2001: American Writers Respond. His work has appeared in over 300 periodicals including *Poetry, American Poetry Review, New Yorker, Southern Review, Kenyon Review, Ontario Review*, and in 200 anthologies.

Karderinis Isidoros was born in Athens. He is a journalist, novelist and poet. He studied economics and completed postgraduate studies in tourism economics. His articles have been published in newspapers, magazines and websites around the world. His poems have been translated into English, French and Spanish and published in poetic anthologies, literary magazines and literary newspaper columns. He has published eight books of poetry and three novels in Greece. His books have been translated and published in the United States, Great Britain, Italy and Spain.

Silvia Kofler is a widely published poet, translator, and educator who has read her work in many places like the Yale Club and Poets House in New York City, and at Schokoladen in Berlin, Germany. Her book *Gambol the World: Eine Weltanschauung*, by Spartan Press has been translated into Portuguese by Carlos Ramos and will be published by Ghost Editions in Portugal.

Věra Kopecká was born in czechoslovakian Turnov and now lives in Broumov. She graduated from pedagogical studies in the field of mathematics at Charles University in Prague. She is a member of the East Bohemian Branch of the Writers' Union (Středisko východočeských spisovatelů) and the Union of (the Czech) Writers (Obec spisovatelů České republiky). She has published 30 poetry books. She published in numerous anthologies in the Czech Republic, Poland and Ukraine. She has participated in international festivals, literary meetings and plein-airs in the Czech Republic, Poland, Slovakia and Greece.

Dimitris P. Kraniotis was born in Larissa Prefecture in central Greece and grew up in Stomio (Larissa). He studied Medicine at the Aristotle University of Thessaloniki, Greece. He lives in Larissa and works as a medical doctor (internal medicine specialist). He is the author of 10 poetry books in Greece and abroad. He is the Editor-in-chief of the international anthology in English "World Poetry 2011" (205 poets from 65 countries). He received international awards for his poetry which has been translated in 34 languages & published in books, anthologies & magazines in many countries around the World.

Maria Lisella is the sixth Queens Poet Laureate; in 2020, who received an Academy of American Poets Laureate Fellowship. Featured on Grace Cavalieri's series, The Poet and the Poem at the Library of Congress, she recently won third prize in the Amilcare Solferini International Literary Competition. Her work appears in Thieves in the Family (NYQ Books), Amore on Hope Street (Finishing Line Press) and Two Naked Feet (Poets Wear Prada). Her new manuscript entitled *The Man with a Plan* is pending publication. She co-curates the Italian American Writers Association readings; and is a contributor to the bilingual La Voce di New York, Never Stop Traveling and The Jerusalem Post.

Roberto Mendoza-Ayala is a poet and publisher from Mexico. In 1994, as a member of the *Nautilium* literary group, he was awarded the FONCA Grant for creative writing. He has published the following books of Poetry: *Las Otras Estaciones* ((1994), *Negraluz* ((2004), and *Ultrasonidos* (2012). He has also published a collection of short stories, *Cerquita de Dios* (2006). His poems, stories and essays have been published in national and international anthologies and magazines. He is the director of Darklight Publishing based in New York.

Tareq Mahmud (1974 – 2023) was a cultural activist, poet, publisher, actor and film maker. He also edited *Pathik*, a literary magazine for 26 years. He wrote more than twenty collections of poetry including *Phire Jacchi Hrider Kachhe, Meghera Dekechhilo Jaini, Subornar Chokh, Bhalobasha Kothati Jebhabe Bola Dorkar, Akash Bole Kichhu Nei, Prepaid Bhalobasha, Periye Jacchi Sokol Doroja* and others. He was a member of the Directors' Guild, Bangladesh and acted in small screen productions, written scripts and directed teleplays and documentaries.

David Mills holds an MFA from Warren Wilson College and an MA from New York University—both in creative writing—as well as a B.A. (cum laude) from Yale University. He's published four poetry collections: *Boneyarn, The Sudden Country, The Dream Detective,* and *After Mistic.* His poems have appeared in *Ploughshares, Colorado Review, Crab Orchard Review, Jubilat, Callaloo, Obsidian, Brooklyn Rail, Diode*

Journal and *Fence*. He has received fellowships from the New York Foundation for the Arts, Breadloaf, The American Antiquarian Society, the Lannan Foundation, Arts Link and a Henry James and Hughes/Diop fellowship. He lived in Langston Hughes' landmark home for three years.

Thomas Möhlmann Is a poet from the Netherlands. He studied Modern Dutch Literature at the University of Amsterdam. He published six collections of poetry in Dutch, and thirteen anthologies in the Netherlands, Macedonia, Argentina, Colombia and England. His most recent collection of poetry was published in 2021: *Grateful Body*, a love story in poems. His poems have been translated and published in thirteen languages and was awarded the Dunya Poetry Prize and the prestigious Lucy B. & C.W. van der Hoogt Prize. He taught creative writing and poetry at the ArtEZ Academy of the Arts in Arnhem and at the Writers Academy Amsterdam. He is now editor of poetry magazine *Awater* and poetry editor at the literary publishers Querido and De Arbeiderspers in Amsterdam.

Barbara Orlowski was born in Toruń. She is a nurse by profession. In 1988, she emigrated to Germany and has since lived in Krefeld. Her poetry has been published in many anthologies in Germany, Poland, England, China and the USA. In 2012 she published the bootleg audiobook titled *Selected Poems*. Her other published books include *Słowami po krawędziach* (With words on the edges, London 2013), *Ostatnie ślady na piasku* (The last traces in the sand of Bydgoszcz 2019), *Kiedy kwiaty całują niebo* (When flowers kiss the sky Bydgoszcz 2020). Winner of many Polish and foreign awards, like Konopnicka Prize, Ianicius Prize, Phoenix Prize, Bolesław Prus Prize, Barbara is member of Chamber of the HOMER–European Medal of Poetry and Art (Brussels) and she is depositary of Medal. She published a lot of poems in England, Belgium, the Netherlands, Poland, Germany and Brazil.

Attila Szabó Palócz is a writer, playwright, novelist, journalist, editor, translator, actor, and a director from the Federal Republic of Yugoslavia, now lives in Hungary. He is one of the founding members of the AIOWA theatrical group. His visual art has been displayed in many countries, including the USA, Cuba, Brazil, Japan, Spain, Greece, Hungary and Yugoslavia. His latest book, *Travels with My Father-in-Law*, was published in 2023 in Budapest. His plays were–and are still–being put on stage by different theatrical companies both in Hungary and in Serbia. He is also regularly translating different literary works, mainly from Southern Slavic and English languages into Hungarian, but on occasion, he also translates from Hungarian into Serbian, Croatian or Bosnian.

Piter Prokopiak is a Polish writer, publicist, and researcher of Bruno Schulz's work. He is a member of the Polish Writers' Union. Author of 6 books of poetry, 3 novels, 3 books of short stories, two of which were translated and published in Ukraine. Participant of international festivals. He has been awarded for outstanding services to Polish culture and for strengthening Polish-Ukrainian cooperation in the field of literature.

Rudy Alfonzo Gomez Rivas is a poet from Guatemala. He has published the poetry books: *Mares en el corazón del perro, Saudade, Arena de la muerte, Minuto cero, Imperecedera muerte, El silencio como invento, Aves de papel, La fría hoguera de las palabras* and *Desheredados inquilinos* in narrative. He has participated in congresses, meetings, book fairs and festivals at national and international level. Director of the literary magazine *Voces Convergentes* and *CAFEÍNA EDITORES* publishing house. Rudy is the founder and Organizer of the Aguacatán International Poetry Festival—FIPA.

Dhee Sankar completed his PhD in literature from Presidency University, Kolkata, India. He writes poetry in English and in Bengali. His debut collection of Bengali poems, *Ushor Pandulipi*, was published by Patra Bharati in 2022. His English poetry and short stories have appeared in *Muse India, Harbinger Asylum, Grand Little Things, Samyukta Fiction, Setu,* and the *Poetry and Covid* archive by the government of UK, among others.

Naznin Seamon is the author of ten books including five collections of poetry, two collections of short stories, and a novel. Her first book of poetry, *Adigonta Bistirnoter Dhala*, was published in February 2000 and was reprinted in 2004. She was the recipient of the Shabdaguchha Poetry Award 2007. *Hollowness on the Horizon* (2015) is a collection of her poetry in English translation, published by Feral Press, New York. She is an ESL teacher for a NYC High School.

Shourav Sikder is a poet and professor of Linguistics at the University of Dhaka, Bangladesh. His poetry has been featured in numerous journals and newspapers. He wrote more than 30 books, including poetry collections, novels, critical essays, and travelogues. Professor Sikder is a frequent world traveler. His most recent book is a travelogue, *Chena Japan Achena Golpo* (Mowla, 2023).

George Wallace (MPH, MFA) is a NYC based poet and spoken word artist with 42 chapbooks, five albums of spoken word poetry streamed worldwide, and an active schedule of appearances in NYC and worldwide, including an appearance in 2023 at the St Augustine Poetry Festival and recent or scheduled appearances at the Medellin Poetry Festival, National Beat Poetry Festival, Lowell Celebrates Kerouac, Turrialba Poetry Festival, Boao Poetry Festival, Silk Road International Poetry Festival, Piacenza Biennale, Human Underground, Athens; and La Cave Cafe in Paris France. As writer in residence at the Walt Whitman Birthplace, he is creator of POETS BUILDING BRIDGES, now in its third season, triangulating groups of poets from different regions of the world.

Iliana Rodríguez Zuleta received a diploma in Creative Writing from the School of Writers of the General Society of Writers of Mexico, Seventh Generation. She has a PhD from the National Autonomous University of Mexico. She was one of the founders of the *Revista Electrónica de Literatura Mexicana* (*Relim*), which in 2000 was recognized by the iBest award as one of the ten best art and culture websites in Mexico. For more than ten years she has collaborated in the *Suplemento Cultural y Literario* of the newspaper *Unión* (informational organ of the Union of Workers of the National Autonomous University of Mexico).

World Poetry Anthology

Edited by
Hassanal Abdullah

Two hundred and twenty-nine poets
from
fifty-nine countries

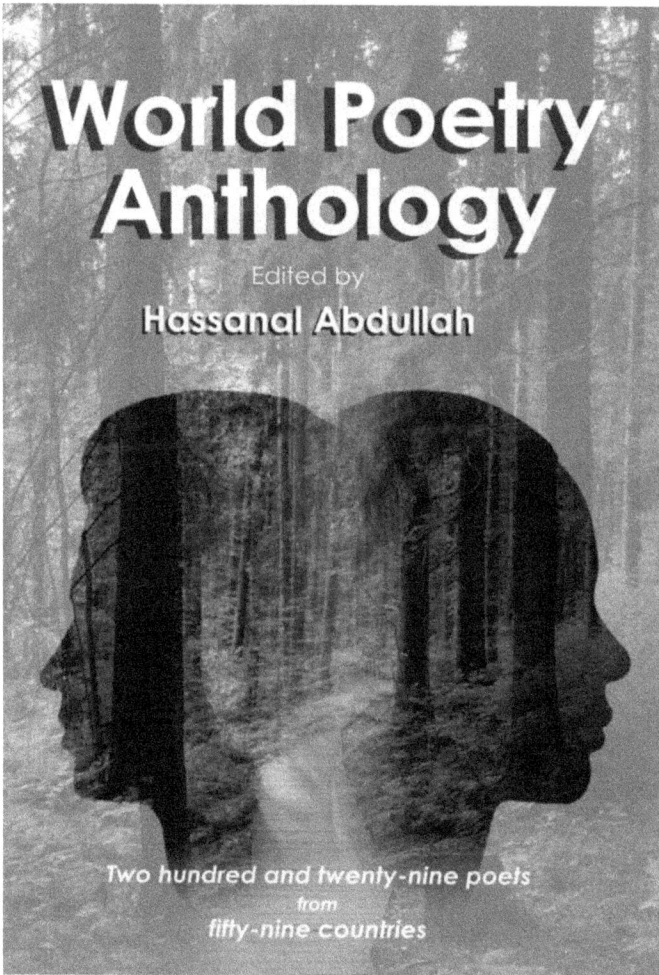

Published by Darklight Publishing (New York-Mexico)
ISBN 979-8-9893407-1-2. Price: $20.00
Available at: amazon.com

"Although I still have a long way to go, what I have read so far surpasses all expectations and the breath and scope of the poets included will certainly rank this anthology among Poetry's Mt Rushmore."—John DeAngelo

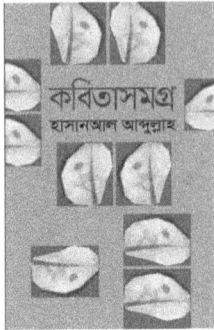

www.ingramcontent.com/pod-product-compliance
Lightning Source LLC
Chambersburg PA
CBHW032051040426
42449CB00007B/1069